STARTING OUT

SKATEBOARDS

LORI DITTMER

CREATIVE EDUCATION • CREATIVE PAPERBACKS

CONT

ENTS

I Am a Skateboard 4

Solo Riding 6

Skateboard Parts 8

Here I Go! 10

Make a Noise 12

Skateboard Words 14

Reading Corner 15

Index 16

I AM A SKATEBOARD.

I roll on paths and ramps.

Look at my deck and my wheels!

I carry one person at a time.

We ride to school or work.
We also ride for fun.

My deck sits on four wheels. Metal trucks connect the wheels.

Ride with one foot, push with the other.

We do tricks sometimes.

My nose pops up. I pull a manny. Whee! Then, my rider drags a foot. We stop.

I stay tucked away until the next ride.

MAKE A NOISE

WHIRRRRR!

Can you make the sounds of a Skateboard? They grind, whoosh, thud, and click.

Listen to these sounds:

Now it is your turn!

SKATEBOARD WORDS

Deck: The flat part of a skateboard that a rider stands on

Manny: A skateboard trick that is like popping a wheelie on a bike

Truck: A metal piece that connects the wheels to the deck

READING CORNER

Bowman, Chris. *Skateboards*. Minneapolis: Bellwether Media, 2022.

Mazzarella, Kerri. *Skateboard* (My First). Coral Springs, Fla.: Seahorse Publishing, 2023.

Schuh, Mari C. *Skateboarding*. Mankato, Minn.: Amicus, 2021.

INDEX

carry 6
foot. 9,11
manny 11
rider 4,11
tricks 10,11
trucks 4,8
wheels 4,8

PUBLISHED BY CREATIVE EDUCATION AND CREATIVE PAPERBACKS
P.O. Box 227, Mankato, Minnesota 56002
Creative Education and Creative Paperbacks are imprints of The Creative Company
www.thecreativecompany.us

LIBRARY OF CONGRESS CATALOGING-IN-PUBLICATION DATA
Names: Dittmer, Lori, author.
Title: Skateboards / by: Lori Dittmer.
Description: Mankato, Minnesota : Creative Education and Creative Paperbacks, [2026] | Series: Starting out | Includes bibliographical references and index. | Audience: Ages 4-7 | Audience: Grades K-1 | Summary: "Introduce beginning readers to a day on the ramps with a skateboard in this STEM starter. Includes photos, a labeled vehicle diagram, "Make a Noise" section, glossary, and further resources"— Provided by publisher.
Identifiers: LCCN 2025013183 (print) | LCCN 2025013184 (ebook) | ISBN 9798895810286 (library binding) | ISBN 9781682779811 (paperback) | ISBN 9798895811542 (ebook)
Subjects: LCSH: Skateboards—Juvenile literature. | Skateboarding —Juvenile literature. | CYAC: Skateboards. | Skateboarding.
Classification: LCC GV859.8 .D58 2026 (print) | LCC GV859.8 (ebook) | DDC 796.22—dc23/eng/20250418
LC record available at https://lccn.loc.gov/2025013183
LC ebook record available at https://lccn.loc.gov/2025013184

DESIGN AND PRODUCTION
Design by Rhea Magaro
Art direction by Graham Morgan

PHOTOGRAPHS BY
Dreamstime/Carlos Carvalho, 2, Lhorib, 6; Getty Images/Jim Rankin, 11, kampee patisena, 5, LOIC VENANCE, 8, ODD ANDERSEN, 4; Pexels/Christian V, 10, Jonathan Portillo, 12; Shutterstock/Refox Photos, cover; Unsplash/Peter Mode, 9; Wikimedia Commons/Cynroya, 14, RSOyama, 7

Printed in the United States